Francis Phillipps.

BLACK BEAUTY

by **Anna Sewell**
re-told by Kay Brown
illustrated by Francis Phillipps

DERRYDALE BOOKS
NEW YORK · AVENEL, NEW JERSEY

CONTENTS

My Early Home   8

Birtwick Park   12

A Stormy Day   16

The Fire   21

Going for the Doctor   24

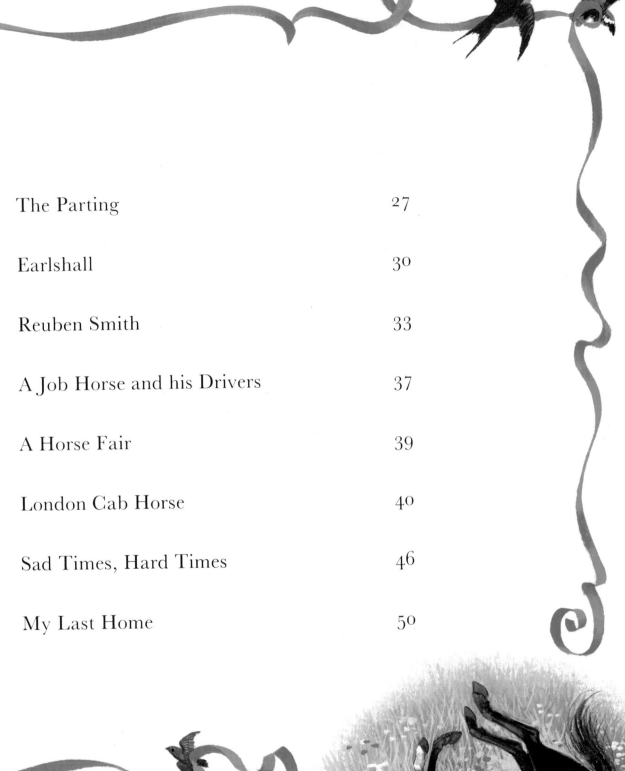

The Parting   27

Earlshall   30

Reuben Smith   33

A Job Horse and his Drivers   37

A Horse Fair   39

London Cab Horse   40

Sad Times, Hard Times   46

My Last Home   50

MY EARLY HOME

The first place I can remember was a large grassy field where I spent happy days galloping and playing with the other foals or resting under the shady trees by the pond. We all belonged to a very kind man, whose special favorite was my mother, and were well looked after. He called me Darkie because I was the only black colt; my mother's name was Duchess.

When I was very young I drank only milk from my mother, because I could not eat grass. She used to work during the day, but always returned to our field in the evening. My mother explained that one day all the young horses would learn to wear harnesses and pull carts but, because I was well-bred—my father and grandfather had both been famous racehorses—I would also be taught to wear a saddle. My mother often talked about the importance of good manners: how I should be gentle and good and never bite or kick. She was a wise old horse.

Sometimes Dick, the farm boy, teased us by throwing sticks to start us galloping. One day our master caught him; he was very angry and told Dick he would lose his job if he ever chased us again! Old Daniel, however, was quiet and kind. He looked after us, teaching us to lead from a headcollar and pick up our feet.

8

When I was nearly two years old something happened which I have never forgotten. It was early spring, with a morning frost on the grass, and my friends and I were quietly grazing when, far away, we heard the noisy crying of dogs. I trotted to my mother, who explained that the sound was hounds hunting. We gathered at the edge of the field, hoping to see the hunt come by. The sound grew louder and louder and we were shaking with excitement! Suddenly a hare rushed by heading for the stream, followed by the hounds and the huntsmen in their bright coats. One by one their glossy horses leapt over the stream . . . but one slipped on the muddy bank and fell into the water. He struggled to his feet, but his rider, covered with mud, lay quite still. I learned later that the dead young man was Squire Gordon's son and that one of the horses had also died that day.

As I grew I became more handsome: my black coat was fine and shining, I had one white foot and a white star on my forehead. When I was four years old Squire Gordon came to look at me; he examined my legs, eyes and mouth and seemed to like me. He then stood by while I walked, trotted and galloped around the field. Finally he said, "When he has been properly broken-in he will suit me very well."

My schooling was about to begin!

The next day my master started my
breaking-in. He put a metal bit in my mouth,
held with straps over my head, then gently placed a saddle on my back. All
the time my master and old Daniel talked to me quietly—and rewarded me
with a carrot when we had finished. This happened every day for a week.
Then, when I was happy to wear the tack, my master got onto my back and
Daniel led me around the field.

It felt very strange at first, but my rider sat still and spoke reassuringly to
me. He rode, without being led, for a little longer each morning until I quite
looked forward to seeing him—and particularly to the tidbit he always gave
me afterwards!

The next, less pleasant, lesson was having my first set of shoes. My master
rode me to the village where the blacksmith had his workshop. There I was
held by a boy while the blacksmith picked up each of my feet in turn, whistling
as he did so, and trimmed back my long hooves with a sharp knife. It didn't
hurt at all. Next there was a lot of noise as the man warmed the iron rods in his
fiery forge, then shaped them with a hammer on an anvil. Sparks flew and

clouds of smoke rose as he tried the hot shoes against each foot, to see if they fitted correctly. When they were cool, the shoes were fixed to my hooves with nails: I jumped at first, but the man was firm and gentle and I soon grew used to the strange feeling and the sound of my new shoes on the road.

When my master considered I was happy and trustworthy being ridden he introduced me to the harness. The bridle had blinkers by my eyes, so I could see only to the front. A heavy padded collar fitted round my neck and a crupper was placed under my tail. I would have kicked out at this, but remembered what my mother had told me when I was very young and soon got used to everything.

My sensible master sent me for two weeks to a neighboring farmer, where I shared a field with some sheep and cows. The railroad ran along one side of this field and I will never forget my first train—a rattling monster shrieked past with no warning and I galloped into the farthest corner where I stood snorting and trembling with fear! Growing-up was indeed a very strange experience.

BIRTWICK PARK

One sunny day, early in May, Squire Gordon's groom came to take me to my new home, Birtwick Park. The grand house was set back from the road up a long drive and the stable yard was neat and clean. I was led into a large, airy loose-box with a deep bed of straw and a rack of sweet-smelling hay. I looked around: tied in a stall next to me was a fat grey pony with a pretty head and dark grey eyes. He said his name was Merrylegs. Beyond him was a fine-looking chestnut: her ears were back and her eyes looked wild. When she went out later Merrylegs told me about her. "Ginger has a habit of biting; she drew blood from James' arm last week and now the young ladies who used to bring us apples and carrots are afraid to come here!" Merrylegs told me that John, the groom, was a kind man, as was James, his helper, and that I would be well looked after at Birtwick Park.

Next morning John groomed me, put on my bridle and saddle and took me for my first outing. We had a splendid gallop on the common! At the Park gates we met Squire Gordon, who asked John how I had behaved.

"First class, sir," said John. "He is willing and fast, but stops with the slightest touch on the reins. He isn't upset by strange sights, or by the rabbit-shooting in the wood. It's clear he has been well-taught."

My new master much enjoyed our ride together the next day— and decided my name should be Black Beauty.

I was happy with my new life at Birtwick Park, although I missed the freedom of the field and the company of the other colts. One day, when Merrylegs was out at exercise, Ginger and I had a long talk about our early lives. When I told her how gently I had been broken-in she seemed very sad: it seems her experience had been quite different.

"It was a bad time for me," she remembered. "Three men dragged me into a corner, wrenched open my mouth and forced a bit into it. I was beaten to make me go forward and shut up night and day. The cruelest of the three was my master's son, Samson: he had a hard voice, a hard eye and a hard hand. It was obvious he only wanted to break my spirit: he would make me work until I could hardly stand. One day I could bear it no longer: the bit in my mouth was agony, Samson's shouts rang in my ears and his whip cut into my neck. For the first time I plunged, kicked and reared . . . all I could think of was trying to get away from that evil man. At last, after a terrible struggle, I threw him off backwards! I heard the thud as he fell to the ground and I galloped to the far corner of the field, where I stood terrified. Slowly, Samson got to his feet and, without even glancing at me,

returned to the house. My sides were bleeding where his spurs had wounded me and I had not eaten for many hours, but the field was bare. I tried to lie down to ease my trembling legs but could not because of the bulky saddle and tight girth.

Many hours later Samson's father came to the field; he spoke to me in his clear, kind voice, took the reins and led me to the stable, where he brought me a bowl of oats. As I ate, he gently sponged the cuts on my body with warm water. I couldn't eat hay, as the harsh stalks hurt my injured mouth, so the old man made a soft, tempting mash of bran and sugar, which I finished gratefully.

After this Samson stayed away and I was nursed back to health by his father and the groom, Tom, before being sold. I had several other homes, some kinder than others, but most of my new owners were rough and thoughtless and I seemed unable to forget the treatment I had had from Samson, until I came here. I really am beginning to trust humans at last."

A STORMY DAY

Later that year, when I was well settled in my new life, I was harnessed ready for a long journey; I enjoyed pulling the light dog-cart for my master and John, the groom. There had been a great deal of rain and the river was swollen and busy; the man at the crossing said the water was rising fast and the forecast was bad. Hearing this, had my master's appointment not been important, we would have returned home.

We got to town, where my master's business took several hours. By the time we headed for home a wild storm was raging: branches snapped in the fierce wind, which made a roaring sound through the trees.

Eventually we came to the river crossing. By this time it was almost dark: foamy water lapped the planks of the bridge and the wind howled. Knowing we were all anxious to be home I did not hesitate, putting my front feet on the bridge. Suddenly I felt a mysterious fear—I stopped, jerking the dog-cart and causing my master to shout out. He urged me forward, gently at first but, when I did not move, he raised his whip. Still, something unseen prevented me from crossing. John was sent to my head to lead me onto the bridge, but I lifted my front legs and refused to move. "Come on Beauty, what's the matter?" cried John above the sound of the storm.

Just then the man who lived in the cottage by the bridge ran up waving a lantern and shouting. "Don't try to cross here!" he cried. "The bridge is broken in the middle and part of it has been washed away—if you step on it you'll be in the river!"

My master turned me gently away and he and John made a great fuss, patting and praising me for having saved them from a disaster.

It grew darker and darker and the wild wind blew in gusts; I trotted smartly along the road while my master and John talked in low, serious voices. It seemed they were sure we would all have drowned had I not stopped as I did! John had many stories to tell of dogs and horses having a 'sixth sense' in moments of danger.

The route home we had to take to avoid the river was very much longer, but we went steadily and covered the miles. John left the reins loose, allowing me to go at my own speed, for the rain had dislodged many large stones and washed them onto the road. Since we had expected to be home before dark, we had only brought one lamp and eerie shadows from the racing clouds made the journey difficult.

Had we been going any faster we would not have escaped an accident for the second time that night. On rounding a bend we found our way blocked by a huge fallen tree, brought down by the gale. I stopped just in time, my hooves sliding in the muddy puddles, causing the cart to tip up. It was clear two men alone would never move the tree, so John went on foot to the nearest farm for help. Luckily the farmer had two strong Shire horses: they put their massive chests into their collars and, with lowered heads, pulled until I thought the chains to the tree trunk would break! Very slowly, with a crashing and cracking we could hear even above the storm, the tree moved. The farmer urged his horses on, while the rain beat down and the thunder rumbled. It took over an hour to clear the obstruction, by which time I was wetter and colder than ever in my life. Thanking the farmer, we continued on our way half expecting to meet another hazard around each corner. The road had become flooded as we neared home, but at last the wind was beginning to die down. You can imagine what a welcome sight were the gates of Birtwick Park . . . and how very glad I was to see my dry stable!

Most of my working days at Birtwick Park were spent at exercise with John, visiting business acquaintances with my master or pulling the carriage with Ginger.

One morning Ginger and I were harnessed early and James, the groom, with my master and mistress, set off to see some friends nearly fifty miles away. Because of the distance we were all to spend the night away from home, which did not happen often.

James drove us well: he allowed us time to catch our breath up the steep hills and used the drag—a sort of brake—expertly on the downward slopes, so that the carriage didn't follow us too fast. However, by the time we arrived at our stopping place—a large hotel in a busy market town—both Ginger and I were quite tired.

We were taken to a quiet stable and brushed over by a tiny man with a wrinkled face and bent legs, who whistled softly while he worked. I have never been groomed so thoroughly yet so quickly! "What a good animal this is," he said to James. "I have been with horses since I was twelve years old and reckon I can tell how each one has been handled. This fellow—'Beauty' you call him—has good manners and a trusting nature. You are a pleasure to care for," he added softly in my ear. James told the old man where we lived: he remembered the hunting accident that had caused the death of Squire Gordon's son. By the time I had a rug on my back and hay in my rack, he and James were firm friends.

THE FIRE

Later in the evening a traveler's horse was brought in by another young groom. While he was brushing the sweating animal a young man with a pipe in his mouth strolled into the stable for a gossip. "Don't stand and watch me work," said the groom. "Run up the ladder into the loft and bring this chap some hay!"

The other lad went, at his own speed, and I heard his footsteps overhead. A few minutes later they both went out and shortly after that—it must have been nearly midnight—James came in to check Ginger and me, locking the door as he left. I don't know how long I was sleeping, but I woke in the night feeling very uncomfortable. I stood up: the air was thick and choking. I could hear Ginger in the next stall coughing and all the other horses moving about restlessly. A sound of crackling and snapping was coming from above us, with a low, rushing noise behind it! I began to sweat and tremble with fear of the unknown. By now we were all awake—and all very frightened.

At last I heard footsteps outside
and the groom who had brought
the traveler's horse burst in. He
began hurriedly to untie the horses
and try to lead them out; however
he was in such a panic and so
obviously terrified himself that none
of them would trust him and they
would not move. He tried to drag
us out by force in turn, but when he
saw it was useless he gave up and
left.

The night air, which was now
rushing in through the open door,
made it slightly easier to breathe
but from behind the dense smoke
I suddenly saw a dancing orange
light and felt burning heat.
Someone outside cried "Fire!" and
the old groom appeared in the
doorway. Calmly he led out each
horse in turn and was nearly by me
when I heard James' voice. "Come
along Beauty, time for us to leave,"
he murmured as he put on my
bridle. Then, tying his neckscarf
lightly around my eyes and patting
and coaxing me all the while, he led
me out onto the yard. Slipping off
the scarf, he called to someone to
take my reins and darted back into
the burning stable. I whinnied
anxiously as I saw him go—and
Ginger told me later that it was the
sound of my voice that made her
able to move to safety with James
through the smoke.

There was a commotion in the
yard by now, with loose horses
slipping on the cobbles and men
rushing past in the dark with
buckets of water. Later, when the
fire was out and men and horses
calm, we left to finish our journey
. . . but I shall always remember
that fearful night.

GOING FOR THE DOCTOR

James left soon after the fire to take up a job as head groom. We all missed him, but life went on as before at Birtwick Park.

One night I was awakened by the sound of John's footsteps on the yard: he burst into the stable with my bridle in his hand and said that we were to go with a note for the doctor as my mistress was very ill. In no time John was on my back and we sped across the park, through the village streets and out into the country. It was a frosty moonlit night and I galloped faster than ever before, covering the miles as quickly as even my grandfather had at Newmarket races! John thought I should stop to recover my breath, but my spirits were up and I did not slow down until we reached the town.

The doctor, raised from sleep, came to the window. "What do you want?" he called down.

"Come quickly," said John. "My mistress is very sick and the Squire has sent this note!"

The doctor looked worried. "My horse has worked all day and couldn't make the journey," he said to John. "May I take yours?"

"I was supposed to rest him, for he has galloped all the way here," explained John, "but if any horse is brave enough to get you there it's Black Beauty." Saying this he patted my sweating neck and, promising to take care of me, the doctor set off to Birtwick. We did stop once on the way home, for I could hardly breathe, and although a thoughtful rider, the doctor was neither as light nor as experienced as John.

Joe, a young lad who had helped since James left, took my reins from the doctor who bounded up the steps to attend his patient. Joe led me to the stable; I was glad to be home for my legs felt weak and I was trembling and steaming. Joe brought me a bucket of cold water and rubbed my legs and chest; he did not put on my rug because he said I was too warm already. Then he left me to rest, but I soon began to shake and shiver with cold. My legs and body ached and every breath I took was painful. How I longed for my thick, warm rug! John would not be back from his eight-mile walk for some time, so I lay down in the straw and tried to sleep.

After a long while I heard John at the door. I was by now in great pain and John seemed to know. He brought me three light rugs and ran back to the house for warm water and an oatmeal drink. John stayed with me that night: I slept fitfully, but he was there each time I woke.

By the next morning I was very ill: my lungs were inflamed, which made breathing difficult, and I was too weak to stand for long. My raised temperature made me feel distant from all that was going on—but I remember John's voice saying crossly, "Stupid boy! No rugs and cold water for a hot horse! He should have known better." He was talking, of course, about Joe.

My master came to see me and spent some time in my stable. It seemed I had brought the doctor to my mistress just in time and, although still very ill, she had improved. Joe, too, often sat near me doing his jobs; he was quiet and seemed unhappy. John's remarks had hurt him, for he had only done what he had thought was best, and he felt responsible for my illness.

Ginger and Merrylegs had been moved to a far stable to give me quiet in which to recover. One evening John and Joe's father, Tom, came to give me my medicine; afterwards they sat on a bale of straw in silence. After a while Tom said, "I wish, John, you'd say a few kind words to Joe. He's very upset, won't eat properly and never smiles." John, patting my neck, said "If Beauty gets better I promise I'll talk to him."

THE PARTING

The next day I felt better and called to John when he came to see me. My legs were stronger and the pain in my chest hurt less. John, however, didn't seem as happy as I thought he would be. It seemed my mistress was still very sick and the doctor had advised her to live in a warm dry climate. The master had decided that day that they should leave Birtwick Park and John had just heard the news.

As I grew stronger, so the packing up and moving of Squire and Mrs. Gordon's home gathered pace. John and Joe, who were once again good friends, tidied the saddle-room and cleaned the carriages. The first to leave was Merrylegs—he was going to the vicar for his wife to drive about the town. Joe was going there too, to help in the house and garden (and look after Merrylegs, of course).

The evening before the family left, Squire Gordon came to see us for the last time, for the next day he would be too busy to say goodbye. He stroked my nose and rubbed my ears. "We owe a great deal to you, Beauty," he murmured gratefully.

The last, sad day had come. Ginger and I brought the carriage to the front door for the last time. The hand luggage, hatboxes, cushions and rugs were loaded. Then my master and mistress appeared—she looking weak and pale in her black silk and holding her husband's arm. He settled her beside him in the carriage, John took up the reins and, with a last look at Birtwick Hall, we moved off down the drive.

As we passed through the village it seemed as though everyone was waiting to say goodbye—indeed, crowds lined the streets all the way to the station. John, his voice gruff with emotion, said farewell to his good master and Joe buried his face in my mane to hide his tears.

Soon the steam engine came clattering and puffing into the station; had John not been beside me I think I would have been frightened.

Ginger and I stood as the luggage was loaded. Several people came to admire us and I was glad my master could be proud of me on this day. There was a great deal of noise and bustle: the huge engine was filled with water and coal and the carriages swept and polished for the next journey.

As I stood beside Ginger I thought back over my years with Squire Gordon. I remembered arriving at Birtwick Park, meeting Merrylegs and Ginger and the first ride my master and I had together, when he decided on my new name. I recalled the night of the storm, when the bridge was damaged, and the fire at the town hotel . . . I could smell again the bitter smoke and hear the flames crackling! More recently, I re-lived the urgent errand John and I had made to fetch the doctor for our poor mistress—who was standing near me on the platform looking so pale and ill.

This was, indeed, the end of an important part of my life.

EARLSHALL

My new home was altogether a much grander place and was called Earlshall
Park. John put me in the care of Mr. York, the coachman, who took Ginger
and me into an airy stable with deep straw beds. He looked us over and told
John, "These seem to be two fine horses, but is there anything I need to know
about them?"

"Well, I'm very sad to part with them both," said John, "but they are quite
unalike. The black has a good nature and always tries to please—he has
never known unkindness and trusts everyone. The chestnut, however, was
cruelly treated before she came to us, although with patience she now behaves
well. But do be careful, for she can show some temper especially if she fears
pain; she is very sensitive to loud voices, flies in summer and harness too
tightly buckled." Mr. York, who had listened carefully, said he would do his
best to see we were well looked after and promised to remember about
Ginger's past. As they were going out of the stable John stopped and said, "I
had better mention we have never used a bearing-rein on any horse: it seems
this was what had most upset the chestnut mare before she came to
Birtwick."

Perhaps I should explain that this piece of harness is used to force horses'
heads into an unnatural position when being driven and, if tightened for long
periods, can be very cruel. It was fashionable for carriage-horses to hold their
heads high—and this was the only reason for its use.

The next day Sir William came to look at us.

"You are as fine as my friend Squire Gordon led me to believe" he said, smiling. Mr. York then recounted what John had told him about the bearing-rein. "Then you must keep an eye on the mare and be sure not to tighten the rein too much, but Lady Isobel will not drive her carriage horses without it," he said.

That afternoon we were groomed and harnessed to the carriage and, as the stable clock struck three, we were led around to the front of the house. It was a much finer place than Birtwick Hall, about four times as big, with servants in uniform standing by the steps. I had blinkers on and could not see behind me, but presently I heard the rustle of silk—and Lady Isobel came to inspect us. She was a tall, proud-looking woman: her expression was haughty and displeased. She said nothing, but got into the carriage and we set off. Mr. York had made sure the bearing-reins were in place, but loose; nevertheless, I felt uncomfortable trying to pull uphill because I couldn't stretch my neck down into the collar. Beside me, Ginger said nothing.

The next afternoon, promptly at three, we were again at the front steps. The silken rustling was heard as the lady came down the steps.

"York!" she said in a cold voice. "You must put these horses' heads higher—they are not fit to be seen."

Mr. York explained, very respectfully, that we had not been reined up for several years and that he thought it best to tighten the rein little by little. He was told to do so immediately, and of course obeyed.

Ginger and I came back that day with aching backs and legs and in low spirits. "Let us hope it goes no tighter," said Ginger wearily. Later that week Lady Isobel came down the steps faster than usual, her dress rustling more than ever. "Get those horses' heads up, I said!" she snapped. "And let's have no more nonsense!" Mr. York looked serious as he drew my head back and fixed the rein, but I stood quietly as I had been taught always to do. Ginger, however, realizing what was about to happen, reared up suddenly and struck out with her front legs, knocking the coachman's hat over his nose and catching me painfully with her shod foot. She continued to plunge and rear, snorting and struggling, until she fell down. Mr. York cried out to one of the footmen to cut Ginger free from the carriage while another servant led me to my stable, where I could still hear the commotion.

Ginger was never used in the carriage again, but was given to Sir William's youngest son to hunt.

REUBEN SMITH

There came a time when the family left for a long stay in London, taking Mr. York with them as coachman. Left in charge of us at Earlshall was Reuben Smith, a very knowledgeable and faithful man whose care of horses was usually excellent. He was particularly good if we were sick or lame, patiently treating us with medicine or poultices for as long as necessary. But Reuben Smith had one problem: he sometimes started drinking and couldn't stop. When drunk, Reuben was a changed character: he was rough, rude and unkind to his family and us, as well as unreliable in his work. This did not happen very often, but had cost him his job more than once—although he had promised Sir William he would never again drink a drop of alcohol, and had kept his promise for several years.

All went well with him until the month before the family was due to return. Colonel Blantyre, on returning to his regiment, paid Reuben handsomely for taking him to the railway station. Reuben was to leave the carriage in town to be repainted, driving me there and having taken my saddle for the ride home. Because of the distance he had been given money to pay for food for us both at the White Lion Hotel. As we made our way there at the end of the afternoon, a nail in one of my shoes worked loose. No one noticed until I had been fed by the hotel's groom, who pointed it out to Reuben Smith. "It'll do 'til we get home," he said in a strange, rough voice. This was unlike him, for the comfort and safety of the horses was always put first at Earlshall. Reuben left, telling the groom we would not be setting off for an hour as he had met some friends in the hotel.

One hour, then two, then three passed and it was almost nine o'clock when Reuben called—in the same, strange voice—for me to be saddled and brought out. He seemed in a very bad temper and shouted at the groom for no reason. As we left the yard the landlord called to Reuben to be careful, but almost before we had left the town streets he gave me a sharp cut with his whip and I galloped for home as fast as I could.

There was little moonlight and the roads were rough now; as we traveled I felt my shoe working loose until, about two miles from the town, it came off altogether. This unfortunately happened just before a stretch of road which had been newly surfaced with large, sharp stones. If Reuben Smith had not been drunk he would have realized something was wrong; as it was he urged me on with threats, shouting and the occasional blow! Over this dark road with a shoe missing at breakneck speed . . . it was only a matter of time before the worst would happen, as it did. As my hoof split and broke so the sensitive part of my foot came into contact with the stones: the pain was too great to bear and I stumbled onto my knees. My rider fell forward as I came down and lay in the road, while I limped to the grassy verge, panting and shaking with pain.

I heard Reuben groan, then try to move, then groan again . . . then all was silent. I could do nothing for him, or even for myself, but I stood still nearby and listened into the darkness for any welcome sound. The road was not used much and all I could hear was the breeze in the grass, a sound that made me think longingly of my days as a foal in the big meadow.

It must have been nearly midnight when, far away, I was sure I heard the sound of a horse's feet! Sometimes it died away, then it grew clearer again, and nearer. Soon I felt sure I recognized Ginger's footsteps! I neighed loudly and, to my joy, Ginger answered. Two men jumped from a cart and ran to the still figure on the road. "It's Reuben!" shouted one. "He's dead—feel how cold his hands are!" They stood for a moment in silence.

Having realized there was no help they could give Reuben, they came to me, noticing my bleeding knees. "The horse fell," said the second man, "and Reuben came off onto his head. It's strange the animal hasn't left—the accident must have happened several hours ago." He then took my reins to lead me: I tried to walk, but almost fell again. "Look!" he cried. "Poor chap—his foot is cut to pieces. No wonder he couldn't go on. If Reuben hadn't had a belly full of beer he'd have noticed his horse had lost a shoe."

The two men carried Reuben's body to the cart, then one tenderly wrapped his scarf over my foot and the sad procession set off, very slowly, for Earlshall.

My injuries healed slowly and no one blamed me for what had happened that night—it was really the drink that caused the death of Reuben Smith.

A JOB HORSE AND HIS DRIVERS

I was to spend several weeks alone in a small field while my foot healed, for I was quite lame. I missed Ginger and thought of her often, calling hopefully when I heard horses' feet passing on the road.

One morning the gate opened and Ginger was led into the field! We were very glad to be together again—but Ginger's story as she told it was not a happy one. She had been ridden hard in the hunting field and raced when she was unfit: as a result her lungs were affected and her back strained. "And so," she said sadly, "here we are in the prime of life, ruined— you by a drunkard and I by a fool."

We spent our days grazing and resting under the trees.

My owner decided I should be sold, for I was scarred from my fall and no longer smart enough for his wife's carriage. I left Ginger early one day and was loaded onto a train for a long, uncomfortable journey to the Southeast of England. There I was met by a young groom who took me to a large stable-yard in the town, where I was tied in a stall and could not turn around. The bedding and food were good, but I was unable to rest properly in my small space.

I had become a 'job horse'—to be hired for driving by anyone who could pay the price. One day a man paid to hire me to take his wife and child out for a drive. I knew right away that he was no horseman: he flopped the reins and waved the whip in a meaningless way, but off I went. We passed a stretch of road which had recently been fixed; there were many loose stones about and any considerate driver would have slowed his horse down at such a place. Mine, however, did not . . . and a stone became stuck between the shoe and one of my forefeet. Needless to say, no one noticed, but I became lamer and lamer until I could barely move forward. My driver then cried out, "I do believe we've paid for a lame horse!—either that or he's plain cunning and doesn't want to work!" Saying this he cut me with the whip and would have continued, but a farmer riding past pointed out the reason for the trouble and removed the stone. If he had not come along I think I could have been lamed for a very long time. I worked as a job horse until the owner became ill and the future of all his horses was in doubt.

A HORSE FAIR

What did happen was that most of us were taken to a horse fair, to be sold to the highest bidder. Here there were all kinds of horses: little fat Welsh ponies like Merrylegs, huge heavy horses for farm work and pulling drays and better-bred riding horses and hunters, like myself, fallen on hard times. Some were obviously well cared for, but others were pitiful to see: thin, with untrimmed feet and matted manes. Many were distrustful of all humans, having been roughly handled or cruelly treated.

We were driven in groups up and down while men looked at the way we moved; they whistled, shouted and prodded us with sticks. There were stalls selling food and beer, merry-go-rounds playing loud music and peddlers shouting their wares, dogs barking and babies crying.

Several buyers looked me over and checked my teeth to see my age, but lost interest when they saw my scarred legs. One man, who spoke softly and smelled of new hay, lingered for a long time looking me up and down. He finally offered twenty-four pounds and fifty pence . . . and I was his. My new owner was a London cab driver.

LONDON CAB HORSE

He was named Jeremiah Baker—Jerry to all his friends—and lived in the City of London. He was married to Polly, had a son, Harry, and a daughter, Dolly. Their's was a happy family, as I realized as soon as we arrived home from the horse fair. Such a welcome and so much smiling and laughter made me feel less tired and uncertain about my future. My stable was roomy and clean and I shared it with a tall, thin horse called Captain, who was no longer in his prime but had obviously once been a proud and important animal. He told me he had belonged to an officer in the Cavalry and had fought in the Crimean War.

Next morning Polly and Dolly brought slices of apple and made a great fuss over me, saying how handsome I was and, had it not been for my scarred knees, far too good for pulling a cab. I must say I enjoyed their attention and compliments. They named me Jack after a previous favorite. That afternoon I was put to the cab; Jerry was very careful to see the collar fitted comfortably and I was happy he did not use the dreaded bearing-rein. We drove a short way to where a line of other cabs were waiting to be hired. The drivers were standing together talking but, when we joined the back of the line, they came to inspect Jerry's new horse. "Right color to pull a funeral hearse," said one.

"Too smart for this job," said another, "there'll be problems with this one, mark my words!"

Jerry seemed unconcerned, until a large man dressed in a grey bowler hat and a grey cape came up: he was the self-appointed leader of the group, having been a cab-owner longer than anyone else. He examined me very thoroughly, then said quietly to Jerry, "I don't know what you paid for him, but he'll be worth every penny!" And so I was accepted in my new life.

I found the first week in London very tiring, for I was not used to the noise, the bustle and the crowds. Threading my way between the rushing traffic made me quite nervous at first but I soon learned I could trust my driver and we worked well as a team. Jerry understood our needs in the stable, too, keeping our beds clean and water fresh. The best day of the week was Sunday, our rest day, when Captain and I spoke of our early lives and past experiences.

Harry used to help by soaping the harness and polishing its brass fittings, while little Dolly and her mother brushed out the cab, beat the seat-cushions and cleaned the windows until they sparkled. They were always laughing together as they worked and Jerry would whistle softly as he groomed me in the yard. That Jerry thought of his horses first was proved one afternoon when two men leaving the hotel demanded to be taken to the station at top speed. Jerry refused their offer of double fare, saying we would take them at the normal speed or not at all. They left in the next cab, whose driver thought little of his exhausted horse and more of his pocket! I was growing very fond of my new master.

Some of the cab-drivers were too poor to own their own horses so rented them daily and drove them hard to pay for them and make a little money for themselves and their families. Jerry would not work on Sundays, saying both he and I were entitled to one day's rest a week, but many of the cab horses were never rested.

Now my work in London's busy streets was second nature: I never thought twice about threading my way between huge drays laden with barrels or hearing rattling handcarts before I could see them. Little ponies were often

used to pull enormous loads—I saw one no bigger than Merrylegs who was doing his best with a heavy cart while the boy driving cut him with his whip. The butcher's horses worked as hard as any, for the cooks in the grand houses ordered meat in great quantities every day and all had to be delivered on time. Fresh fruit and vegetables, fish, milk and bread—all were moved from here to there by horses and, sometimes, donkeys. Should a fire engine be called out there was a strong team of fast horses to pull it; when someone important died he was taken to his grave by a pair of high-stepping black horses with black feather plumes on their heads. London was, indeed, full of horses.

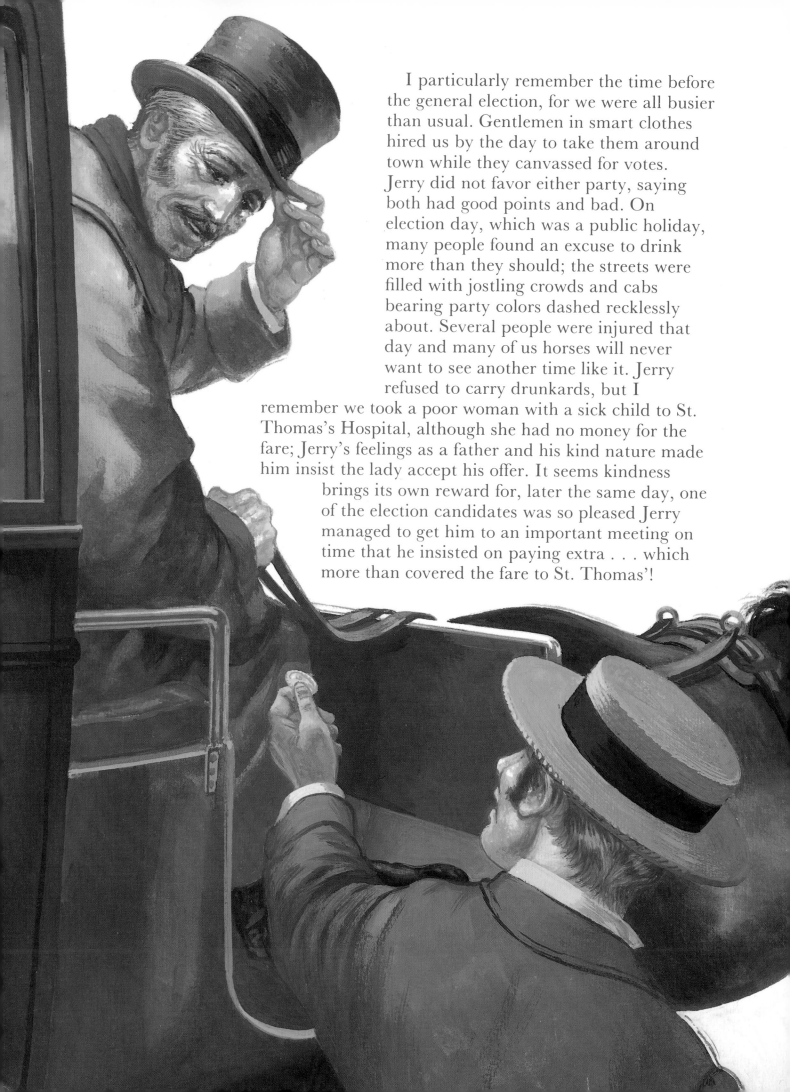

I particularly remember the time before the general election, for we were all busier than usual. Gentlemen in smart clothes hired us by the day to take them around town while they canvassed for votes. Jerry did not favor either party, saying both had good points and bad. On election day, which was a public holiday, many people found an excuse to drink more than they should; the streets were filled with jostling crowds and cabs bearing party colors dashed recklessly about. Several people were injured that day and many of us horses will never want to see another time like it. Jerry refused to carry drunkards, but I remember we took a poor woman with a sick child to St. Thomas's Hospital, although she had no money for the fare; Jerry's feelings as a father and his kind nature made him insist the lady accept his offer. It seems kindness brings its own reward for, later the same day, one of the election candidates was so pleased Jerry managed to get him to an important meeting on time that he insisted on paying extra . . . which more than covered the fare to St. Thomas'!

I have told you that Jerry always spent Sundays at home, going to church in the morning and enjoying time with his family. Early one May Sunday Jerry was grooming me in the yard when Polly rushed up. "Poor Dinah Brown has just had a letter saying her mother is dangerously ill and she must go to her straight away. Her mother lives about ten miles from here, right out in the country: Dinah cannot walk far as she has recently given birth to her youngest child. I know none of us likes you working on a Sunday, but I keep thinking of how I'd feel if I couldn't get home at a time like this . . ." Jerry, of course, felt just the same and, having borrowed the butcher's light trap which was much easier to pull than our cab, we set off.

It was a fine spring morning and we had soon left the town far behind; the sweet air, smell of the new grass and the empty country lanes made me feel refreshed. When we arrived at the farm Jerry asked if I might be turned out in their small meadow with the two cows. Oh, the feeling of having no harness, of being able to roll on the soft ground and pick at the fresh grass in the sunshine! Jerry sat down under a tree to watch and eat the lunch Polly had packed for him. It was a Sunday to remember!

SAD TIMES, HARD TIMES

One winter's evening I met Ginger again—but I hardly recognized the worn out chestnut with a sad face and bones sticking through her thin coat. She had been sold many times and was now sick and waiting to die. We talked of the old days, but I could say nothing to comfort her and left her standing forlornly in the icy rain. I have never felt so sad or helpless.

Christmas and New Year are happy times for most people, but for cabmen and their horses there was no holiday. One New Year's Eve we took two gentlemen to an elegant house in London's West End. We left them at nine o'clock and were told to return at eleven. "You may have to wait a few minutes," said one, "as we're playing cards, but don't be late." Jerry was always punctual and we were outside the house again on the stroke of eleven. We waited, hearing a clock chime every quarter of an hour: still no one came. The sleet fell straight down, my legs were numb with cold and Jerry was coughing almost non-stop. At half past midnight he rang the bell and asked if we were still needed. "Oh yes," said the servant, "they shouldn't be long now, but you must wait." At quarter past one the two men reappeared, but there was no apology for keeping us waiting so long.

When we at last reached home Jerry could hardly speak and I was shaking with cold. Polly, who had watched anxiously at the window, helped her husband into the house and sent Harry to make me comfortable with extra straw and a warm mash to eat. He dried my back and legs, but did not chatter or whistle—I knew he was worried about his father.

No one came to the stables until quite late the next morning; Harry fed us and mucked us out, but we were not groomed ready for work. The next time Harry came, Dolly was with him: she was crying. It seemed their father was dangerously ill with bronchitis. The leader of the cabmen came to see how Jerry was and offered to work his other horse and bring back half the money—for in those days there was no income if no work was done. He thought I would be all right if Harry led me out each day, but the new horse Hotspur (Captain had recently been retired) was not so sensible and needed to work regularly. He came for Hotspur for about ten days and, as he promised, brought back some earnings for the family. Gradually, Jerry's health improved—but the doctor told him he could never go back to his old job. However, the family's luck changed: a lady living in the country heard Jerry had no work and wrote to ask if he would be her coachman, with Polly to help in the house. There would be a cottage for them all, work for Harry later and a school nearby for Dolly. Everyone was very excited—but this meant I would have to be sold yet again.

I shall never forget my next master. He had hard, black eyes and a broken nose; his mouth was full of discolored teeth and his voice loud and harsh. His name was Nicholas Skinner—and he was unfit to own horses. All that mattered to Mr. Skinner was making money: how his horses suffered while he did this was not important. His cabs were heavy and old, the harness poorly looked after; our food was the cheapest and not sufficient for the work we were expected to do. There was never a day's rest and we were pulled out of our dark, damp stable at any time of the night or day to be driven hard and thoughtlessly. After a fortnight with Nicholas Skinner my bones showed through my flesh and my spirit was broken.

One morning, when I had already worked several hours without food, we had to take a family to the station. They had a lot of heavy luggage and were in a hurry. I did my best and managed to keep going until the steep slope of Ludgate Hill: my feet slipped from under me and I lay exhausted in the road. I was sure I was going to die. I heard someone say, "He'll never get up again!" and felt Skinner's rough hands taking off my harness. I must have been lying in the road for several hours, but at last felt able to stand and was led to a nearby stable. In the evening a veterinary surgeon came, with Skinner, to examine me: he said the best plan was to feed and rest me until the next horse sale, when I might fetch a few pounds.

MY LAST HOME

To my surprise, twelve days of good food and rest made me feel almost well again and I arrived at the sale looking more like the horse I once had been. Most of the others there were poor creatures—lame, scarred, broken-winded or very old—and the men buying were a rough crowd after a bargain. When I had stood tied up for the best part of the morning a farmer and his son came to look; he was softly spoken and his manner was gentle. "There's a horse, William, that has known better days," he said, stroking my neck. On seeing some interest the dealer who was selling me for Mr. Skinner told the farmer what had happened to me through over-work. "But his wind is good and he's a pleasure to handle," he said. "If you want him, he's yours for five pounds!" The man watched me trot up, inspected my teeth and then, to William's great delight, paid over his money.

I was ridden later that day to Mr. Thoroughgood's home just outside the town and turned loose in a large field with a shelter in one corner. William was asked to look after me and seemed very proud of his new responsibility.

He came to check me every day, bringing carrots and oats, and I followed him about the field.

After several months of complete rest I had put on some flesh and my coat had become shiny and soft; I felt quite young again. Mr. Thoroughgood thought I was ready for some light work—he was pleased with my easy paces and I enjoyed going out with him and William.

One summer morning the groom brushed me carefully, trimmed my heels and oiled my feet. It was obviously a special day. William harnessed me to the light carriage and we set off. About two miles from the village we stopped at a pretty house with a neat garden; William rang the bell and asked if the ladies were at home. Three sisters lived there: they had asked Mr. Thoroughgood to find them a good driving horse and he had suggested me.

Seeing my scarred knees the elder sister was about to send me home, but Mr. Thoroughgood pointed out that many fine horses are brought down by bad driving and persuaded the ladies to take me for a week's trial. A groom led me to their stable and left me to settle in. The following morning, as he brushed my face, I heard him murmur, "This is just like the star Black Beauty had . . . I wonder what happened to him?" As he groomed me he muttered, "And one white foot, the little patch of white hairs on his neck—It must be him! Beauty—Black Beauty—it's me . . . little Joe Green who almost killed you through ignorance!" And he began patting and hugging me, saying my old name over and over again. I cannot honestly say I recognized Joe, for the boy had become a man with a mustache and deep voice, but I was sure he knew me and so was happy. Joe told the ladies and, as the week continued, I did my best not to let him down. When the trial was over the sisters bought me—and changed my name back to Black Beauty.

I have now lived here for over a year, with Joe and the ladies. William comes to see me often and I could not be happier. So my story ends—in an orchard like the one at Birtwick, dreaming, with my friends, under the apple trees.

This 1993 edition published by Derrydale Books,
distributed by Outlet Book Company, Inc.,
a Random House Company, 40 Engelhard Avenue,
Avenel, New Jersey 07001

Random House
New York · Toronto · London · Sydney · Auckland

Printed and bound in Singapore

ISBN 0-517-08777-4